20 WAYS TO COOK CHOCOLATE

Lin Chapman is co-owner, with Geoff her Canadian chef husband, of Le Petit Canard - a small and highly acclaimed restaurant. The two of them are also authors of the book on soups in this series.

20 Ways to Cook
CHOCOLATE

Lin Chapman

Thomas Harmsworth Publishing Company

First Published 1994 by
Thomas Harmsworth Publishing
Company
Old Rectory Offices
Stoke Abbott
Beaminster
Dorset DT8 3JT
United Kingdom

British Library Cataloguing-in-Publication
Data. A catalogue record for this book is
available from the British Library.

ISSN 1355-4050
ISBN 0 948807 24 5

Printed and bound in Great Britain by
BPC Paulton Books Ltd

CONTENTS

INTRODUCTION

Just the sound of the word - *chocolate* - evokes deep, primeval yearnings for the taste and texture in your mouth - sweetly sensual, silky-smooth, and melting. It is devilishly wicked, yet simultaneously comforting, and it satisfies in a way that few other foods can.

THE BASIS OF THE CHOCOLATE WE EAT

Chocolate derives from cocoa beans. Each pod from the Cocoa tree contains up to 30 small beans which are fermented, roasted, shelled and pressed, producing cocoa liquor and cocoa butter. These two elements, known as cocoa solids are stirred with sugar, flavourings (generally vanilla) to give us chocolate as we know it. The percentage of cocoa solids determines the quality and depth of flavour of the final product.

TYPES OF CHOCOLATE

Chocolate appears in many guises - dark, milk and white - and levels of quality - couverture, bakers and confectionery.

 1

Couverture or professional chocolate is the very best available. Dark couverture generally contains 55 - 75% cocoa solids, pure vanilla, little sugar and has silk-like texture, intense flavour and a glossy, refined finish. It is available as bitter, dark, milk and white.

Due to the different melting and setting points of the complex fats in couverture it is necessary to 'temper' the chocolate to achieve a perfect, glossy finish. For the purposes of this book only two recipes require tempering - Chocolate Glaze (page 68) and Chocolate Garnishes (page 36). See instructions for chocolate tempering on page 4.

Couverture is generally sold through specialist wholesalers to up-market restaurants, bakers and chocolatiers. You may find couverture in a specialist food store, if not you might approach one of the above for guidance or the contacts given at the back of the book. Other sources might be top department store food halls. Although it is not as widely available, it is possible to buy pre-tempered couverture.

Couvertures to seek out:
Valrhona, 'Grand cru' chocolates and probably the finest available.
Cocoa Barry has a wide range of styles including pre-tempered.
Callebaut and Patisfrance.

Bakers Chocolate requires no tempering as most of the cocoa butter is replaced by vegetable oil. This produces a chocolate that is easy to use but with much less flavour than couverture. It is available in dark (semi-sweet), milk and white

 2

and can be found in better supermarkets and speciality food stores.

Confectionery chocolate is the cheapest and most adulterated form of chocolate available.

Most or all of the cocoa butter is replaced by vegetable fats and it as blended with artificial flavouring, a higher proportion of sugar and possibly milk powders. For the recipes in this book good quality plain confectionery chocolate may be used but do read labels and seek out a reputable chocolate minimum 48% cocoa solids. Milk and white confectionery chocolate is not suitable for cooking as they are too adulterated to melt well and have little true chocolate flavour. Regulations in some countries do not allow the addition of vegetable fats so chocolate from, for example, France, Belgium and Switzerland is likely to have a high quantity of cocoa solids.

White chocolate has no cocoa liquor, which imparts colour to other chocolates, is very sweet and has a waxy texture.

Milk chocolate has less cocoa solids and therefore a less pronounced flavour than dark chocolate and is blended with milk powders for a creamier texture and flavour.

Cocoa powder (not sweetened drinking chocolate) is derived from cocoa liquor which is dried and desiccated.

 3

STORING CHOCOLATE

Ideally chocolate should be stored in a dry, well-ventilated area with a stable temperature of about 68F/20C. Unused chocolate should be re-wrapped in foil.

MELTING CHOCOLATE

Chocolate melts best chopped finely and placed in the top of a double-boiler over a small amount of barely-simmering water. You can improvise a double boiler by using a stainless steel bowl that fits snugly into the top of a saucepan without touching the water below. Do not attempt to melt chocolate directly over a heat source as it will quickly burn.

TEMPERING CHOCOLATE

You will require a double boiler and a sugar thermometer.

Chop the chocolate finely and melt half of it in the top of a double-boiler stir the melted chocolate until it reaches 118F/48C then remove top of boiler from the heat and immediately stir in the remaining chocolate until it is fully melted and the temperature has dropped to 80F/27C. Return to the heat and, stirring continually, re-heat the chocolate to 88F/31C. Remove from heat and continue to stir for one minute.

The chocolate is now tempered and ready for use.

GRATING CHOCOLATE

Effortless chocolate grating method: chill choc-

4

olate for 1 hour before using and then process in
food processor with metal blade until fine.

 5

IMPERIAL/METRIC CONVERSIONS

Dry weight		Liquid measure	
ounces	grams	fluid ounces	millilitres
1	25	1	25
2	50	2	50
3	75	3	75-90
4 (¼ lb)	125	4	125
5	150	5 (¼ pint)	150
6	175	6	175
7	200	7	200
8 (½ lb)	225	8	225
9	250	9	250
10	275	10 (½ pint)	275
11	300	11	300
12 (¾ lb)	350	12	350
13	375	13	375
14	400	14	400
15	425	15 (¾ pint)	425
16 (1 lb)	450	16	450
17	475	17	475
18	500	18	500
2¼ lb	1000 (1 kilo)	20 (1 pint)	550
		1¾ pints	1000 (1 litre)

6

TABLE OF OVEN TEMPERATURES

	Fahrenheit (F)	Celsius (C)	Gas mark
	150	70	
	175	80	
	200	100	
Very cool	225	110	¼
	250	120	½
	275	140	1
Cool	300	150	2
Warm	325	160	3
Moderate/ Medium	350	180	4
Fairly Hot	375	190	5
	400	200	6
Hot	425	220	7
	450	230	8
Very hot	475	240	9
	500	260	9

CHOCOLATE PECAN PIE

Serves: 8
Preparation time: 20 minutes
Cooking time: 45 minutes
Setting time: 30 minutes
Suitable for dinner party: yes
Suitable for freezing: no
Special equipment: 9 inch (22.5 cm) pie dish

The quintessential North American dessert. Decadent and comforting, the ultimate reward after a 2 hour work-out.

 8

3 eggs
8 oz (225 gm) dark brown sugar
6 oz (175 gm) golden syrup
2 teaspoons vanilla extract
4 oz (125 gm) butter, lightly salted, melted, cooled
8 oz (225 gm) plain, light flour
4 oz (125 gm) pecan halves
4 oz (125 gm) chocolate (dark or milk), chopped
2 tablespoons Bourbon, optional
To make the pastry:
6 oz (175 gm) flour
3 oz (75 gm) butter

To make the *pastry* sift the flour into a bowl. Chop the butter into the flour and mix it gently with your fingers until the mixture resembles breadcrumbs. Line the 9 inch (22.5 cm) pie dish with the pastry and chill for a minimum of 1 hour.

Preheat oven to 325F/160C/gas mark 3. Move the rack to the middle of the oven.

Lightly beat the whole eggs in a bowl. Add the sugar, syrup, vanilla and butter and mix well. Sift in the flour, add the pecans, the chopped chocolate and Bourbon. Stir until fully incorporated.

Bake the pastry shell blind (lined with foil and filled with baking beans or dry rice) for 15 minutes.

Remove the weighted foil and continue baking for a further 10 minutes empty.

Remove the pie shell from the oven and pour in the filling.

  9

Return to the oven and continue baking for 25 minutes until the filling is puffed and golden. The filling will set as it cools.

Leave the pie in the dish to cool and set for at least 30 minutes before slicing.

To serve:
☆ Serve warm (not hot) or at room temperature with a blob of whipped cream or a scoop of vanilla ice cream.

Chef's tips:
☆ Covered and chilled, this pie will keep well for up to a week. Reheat for 5 minutes in a warm oven.

☆ Dark, milk or even white chocolate can be used in this recipe. Adjust sugar slightly if white chocolate is used as it is quite sweet.

 11

CHOCOLATE CAKE WITH CARAMEL MASCARPONE FILLING

Serves: 10
Preparation time: 30 minutes
Cooking time: 25 minutes
Cooling and assembly time: 45 minutes
Suitable for dinner party: yes
Suitable for freezing: no
Special equipment: two 9 inch (22.5 cm) spring-
   form cake tins

Rich, moist chocolate cake surrounding lush, sexy, caramel-flavoured mascarpone. This is a cake that won't be sitting around for long!

 12

Chocolate cake:

10 oz (275 gm) dark chocolate, coarsely chopped
6 large eggs, separated
6 oz (175 gm) butter
6 oz (175 gm) castor sugar
2 oz (50 gm) light (cake) flour

Filling:

4 oz (125 gm) sugar
2 fl oz (50 ml) water
4 fl oz (125 ml) double cream
one 9 oz pack (250 gm) Mascarpone*

To make the *cake*. Butter the cake tins and cut circles of silicone paper to fit the bases.

Preheat the oven to 325F/160C/gas mark 3.

Melt the chocolate and the butter over barely-simmering water.

In a large bowl beat the egg yolks and 5 oz (150 gm) of the sugar until it doubles in volume - approximately 5 minutes.

Add the melted chocolate and stir well until fully incorporated. Fold in the flour.

In a clean bowl beat the egg whites and the remaining 1 oz (25 gm) sugar until soft peaks form.

Carefully fold the egg white into the chocolate mixture. (You may find it easier to incorporate if you mix a little of the chocolate mixture into the whites first.)

Divide the cake batter between the two cake tins and bake in the centre of the oven for about 25 minutes. (The cakes will rise quite a bit but

 13

will fall back towards the end of baking.) When ready the cakes should be very moist in the centre, almost mousse-like and just springy to the touch - they will set whilst cooling. Remove the cake tins from the oven and leave to cool slightly.

After 10 minutes, run a knife around the sides and remove the springforms. Slide the cakes, leaving the paper attached, onto a cooling rack.

Meanwhile prepare the *filling*.

In a heavy-bottomed saucepan bring the sugar and half the water to the boil over a moderate heat. Continue to boil until a golden caramel colour is achieved (275F/140C on a sugar thermometer). Immediately remove from the heat and add the remaining water and the cream, stir-

ring until the liquid is completely calm. Be very cautious at this stage. The caramel will be *extremely hot* and the liquid will boil up angrily when the cream is added. (Use a long-handled spoon to stir in the cream and keep body parts well away from the pan!)

Allow the caramel in the pan to cool to room temperature.

When the caramel has cooled completely, it should be the consistency of heavy syrup. If it has hardened, return the pan to the heat, stirring, for a few seconds. Lightly beat the Mascarpone in a bowl, add the caramel and beat briefly until incorporated.

Reserve chilled until required.

Assembly: Carefully peel the silicone paper from the cakes and place one on a serving plate or cake stand. Spread the caramel Mascarpone evenly over the cake, ½ inch (1.25 cm) from the edge. Place the other cake on top and just before serving dust the top with confectioners' sugar or chocolate glaze (see page 65, Chocolate Pâté recipe).

Chef's tip:

☆ Mascarpone is available from better supermarkets. It is wickedly rich Italian cream, actually classified as dessert cheese due to its high butter fat content. If not available you can substitute double or whipping cream.

CHOCOLATE TIRAMISU

Serves: 6
Preparation time: 25 minutes
Setting time: 4 hours
Waiting time: up to 8 hours
Suitable for dinner party: yes
Suitable for freezing: no
Special equipment: shallow 9 - 10 inch (22.5 - 25 cm) serving dish

A variation on the classic Italian dish, Tiramisu, which means pick-me-up . Despite the richness of the ingredients this velvety, smooth dessert is light and surprisingly uplifting at the end of a meal. Be warned - it is incredibly addictive!

 16

3 eggs, separated
3 oz (75 gm) icing sugar
9 oz (250 gm) pack Mascarpone*
3 tablespoons grated chocolate
1 pack ladyfinger biscuits
1½ fl oz (35 ml) dark rum
1½ fl oz (35 ml) coffee or chocolate liqueur
2½ fl oz (65 ml) strong, brewed coffee

In a large bowl beat the egg yolks and the sugar until pale and thick - about 5 minutes.

Add the Mascarpone, rum and chocolate liqueur and beat on a low speed until smooth.

In a separate bowl beat the whites, with a pinch of salt, until stiff, then fold the whipped whites and the grated chocolate into the cream mixture.

Arrange the ladyfingers in a shallow dish and pour the coffee evenly over them so that all the biscuits are soaked. Spread the cream over the top and refrigerate for 4 to 8 hours.

Garnish the dish with chocolate curls, or Caraque (see page 36) or a light dusting of cocoa powder.

Chef's tips:
☆ For a special presentation - assemble individual Tiramisu desserts in pretty glasses.
Begin with a little of the soaked sponge, then a layer of cream mixture. Repeat the 2 layers and chill until required.
☆ Any chocolate - dark, milk or white can be used in this dish.
☆ Plan to make this dish several hours before serving as it will be at its best after 4 - 6 hours in the fridge.
* Mascarpone is available from better supermarkets.

PEAR & CHOCOLATE STRUDEL

Serves: 3 or 4 small portions
Preparation time: 15 minutes
Cooking time: 25 minutes
Waiting time: 30 minutes
Suitable for dinner party: yes
Suitable for freezing: uncooked
Special equipment: baking sheet, silicone paper,
   pastry brush

Don't be intimidated by Phyllo pastry if you
haven't used it before. It's dead easy, once you
know how, and opens up a whole new world of
cookery. In this recipe crisp, flaky Phyllo pastry
is layered with soft pear and melting chocolate -
a classic marriage of flavours.

 19

14 oz (400 gm) firm, ripe pears e.g. Conference or Anjou
1 oz (25 gm) butter
1 - 1½ oz (25 - 35 gm) castor sugar
½ teaspoon vanilla
7 oz (200 gm) Ricotta cheese
2 tablespoons currants or sultanas soaked in a few drops of rum
pinch nutmeg
3 - 4 oz (75 - 125 gm) chocolate, finely chopped
3 sheets Phyllo pastry - 16 inches x 12 inches (40 x 30 cm)
icing sugar for dusting

Peel and quarter the pears and cut into ½ inch (1.25 cm) cubes. Add all the ingredients, except the butter, and mix gently but thoroughly.

Remove the Phyllo pastry from the sealed package. Unfold and lay the sheets flat on a clean, dry work top. Cover with a clean, damp, tea towel or cloth.

Melt the butter.

Lay the sheet of silicone paper with the long side facing you. Remove one sheet of Phyllo from under the damp towel and lay it over the paper.

Brush the pastry lightly with melted butter. Layer 2 more sheets of Phyllo in this fashion, brushing each with the melted butter.

Mound the pear mixture along the long side facing you, leaving 2 inches (5 cm) uncovered at each end.

Using the silicone paper to help you lift, roll the strudel away from you, quite tightly. Finish

 20

with the seam underneath and fold the ends neatly under as if securing the ends of a package.

Carefully lift the strudel onto a baking sheet and brush the top with melted butter.

Bake in the centre of a preheated oven - 375F/ 190C/gas mark 5 for 20 to 25 minutes or until golden. Allow to cool on the baking sheet before serving dusted with icing sugar.

 21

Chef's tips:

☆ Unused Phyllo should be re-rolled and wrapped tightly in plastic wrap. It can be stored in the fridge for several days. Uncooked, the strudel can be frozen for up to 1 month.

☆ Use less sugar for white chocolate which is sweeter than dark chocolate.

☆ We use 2 inch (5 cm) house painting brushes for super-quick pastry brushing.

WHITE & DARK CHOCOLATE MOUSSE TORTE WITH ORANGE SAUCE

Serves: 10 - 12
Preparation time: dark cake - 20 minutes, white
   mousse - 15 minutes
Cooking time: 30 minutes
Setting time: minimum 4 hours
Suitable for dinner party: yes
Suitable for freezing: yes
Special equipment: 9 inch (22.5 cm) springform
   cake tin, base lined with silicone paper

A unique cake with a cooked mousse-like, flour-less, dark chocolate base and an airy fresh white chocolate mousse topping.

23

Dark chocolate cake:
1 lb (450 gm) dark chocolate, chopped
2 tablespoons instant espresso granules
6 egg yolks
2 egg whites
4 oz (125 gm) sugar
1 teaspoon vanilla extract
8 fl oz (225 ml) double cream
White chocolate mousse:
14 oz (400 gm) white chocolate, chopped
16 fl oz (450 ml) double cream
Orange Sauce:
8 fl oz (225 ml) fresh squeezed orange juice
rind of 1 scrubbed orange, finely sliced
1 fl oz (25 ml) Cointreau or Grand Marnier

To make the *chocolate cake* preheat the oven to 350F/180C/gas mark 4.

Melt the chocolate, the instant espresso mixed with 3 tablespoons of water and leave to cool slightly.

In a large bowl beat the yolks, the egg whites, sugar and vanilla for 2 minutes. Add the chocolate and continue whisking for 1 minute.

In a separate bowl whisk the cream until soft peaks form. Fold the cream into the chocolate mixture.

Pour the batter into the prepared cake tin and bake in the centre of the oven for around 25 minutes or until just set and the sides start to come away from the sides of the pan.

Place the cake tin on a rack to cool.

 24

Meanwhile make the *white chocolate mousse*. Melt the white chocolate and leave until cool but still liquid.

Beat the double cream just until soft peaks form.

Fold the cream into the cooled chocolate. Spread the white mousse over the chocolate cake and chill for several hours or overnight.

To make the *orange sauce* bring the juice and

 25

rind to the boil in a non-reactive saucepan and simmer until the liquid has reduced by half. Add the liqueur and simmer for 30 seconds longer. Remove from the heat. Allow to cool, and store chilled until required.

To serve:
☆ Run a thin knife around the inside of the springform before releasing. Place a wedge of mousse cake on the plate and surround it with a drizzle of orange sauce.

Chef's tip:
☆ If this cake seems too big for your needs you can scale the recipe down by halving the quantities, using a terrine mould, lined with greaseproof paper, instead. Reduce the cake cooking time by 5 to 8 minutes.

HOT POLAR BEAR CHOCOLATE

Serves: 2
Preparation time: 5 minutes
Cooking time: 5 minutes
Suitable for dinner party: not really
Special equipment: none

There used to be a tradition in Vancouver, Canada, that each January 1st at around 10 am, people came from all over town to take part in the New Year's Day Polar Bear Swim at English Bay. Wild costumes were *de rigueur;* and all of those crazy or hung-over enough to actually complete the swim, in near freezing water, were rewarded with a steaming mug of Polar Bear Chocolate, complements of the nearby English Bay Café. Sadly, the restaurant has now gone and I am sure much of the incentive to enter the icy bay has gone with it.

 27

10 fl oz (275 ml) full fat milk	
4 oz (125 gm) dark chocolate, chopped	
2 fl oz (50 ml) Grand Marnier	
2 fl oz (50 ml) Crème de Cacao or other chocolate (or coffee) liqueur	
For a garnish:	
4 tablespoons double cream	
2 teaspoons icing sugar	

Make sure you have the *garnish* ready before you pour the chocolate. For the garnish, whip a little cream with just a sprinkle of icing sugar until soft peaks form.

Gently heat the milk until hot but not boiling, remove from heat and add the chocolate, stirring constantly, until the chocolate has melted. Return to the heat for a few seconds.

Pour half of each of the liqueurs into each of 2 mugs, or Irish Coffee glasses, and fill almost to the top with the hot chocolate. Spoon cream onto the top and dust with chocolate shavings or cocoa powder.

 29

WHITE CHOCOLATE MOUSSE WITH STRAWBERRIES

Serves: 4 - 6
Preparation time: 30 minutes
Setting time: 2 hours
Suitable for dinner party: yes
Suitable for freezing: no
Special equipment: none

It is worth seeking out the very best quality white chocolate for this mousse. Raspberries or a mixture of fresh berries would be equally delicious with the mousse.

 30

5 oz (150 gm) white chocolate, chopped
2 oz (50 gm) unsalted butter
3 large eggs, separated
1 oz (25 gm) icing sugar
8 fl oz (225 ml) whipping cream
pinch cream of tartar
1 lb (450 gm) ripe strawberries, hulled

In a heavy-bottomed saucepan over a low heat melt the butter and the chocolate, stirring constantly. Remove from the heat and leave to cool.

Beat the egg yolks and sugar in a bowl until pale. Transfer the mixture to the top of a double boiler (or a metal bowl over a saucepan of simmering water) and cook whilst whisking for a few minutes until the mixture thickens.

Pour the egg mixture back into a bowl, add the chocolate and beat together until smooth.

Beat the cream until stiff and gently fold into the chocolate mixture.

In a clean bowl beat the egg whites with the cream of tartar until stiff peaks appear. Fold the whites carefully into the mousse.

Chill the mousse, covered, for at least 2 hours before serving.

☆   ☆   ☆

To serve:
☆ Garnish with the strawberries halved, or slice the fruit and fold it into the mousse just prior to serving.

 31

Chef's tip:
☆ If the strawberries are not totally sweet and ripe try slicing and marinating them for 30 minutes with a few drops of Cointreau or other orange-based liqueur.

OLD FASHIONED WALNUT-CHOCOLATE CHIP OATMEAL COOKIES

Makes: 10 big or 20 regular sized cookies
Preparation time: 5 - 10 minutes
Cooking time: 12 minutes
Suitable for dinner party: no
Suitable for freezing: yes, uncooked
Special equipment: food processor

These yummy cookies seem to hit all the pleasure buttons. Melting, rich blobs of chocolate, crunchy nut morsels, crisp on the outside yet moist and chewy in the centre. I make these about the size of small tea plates and nibble on one cookie as a mid-afternoon snack.

 33

8 oz (225 gm) light flour
½ teaspoon baking powder
½ teaspoon baking soda
4 oz (125 gm) butter, softened
4 oz (125 gm) granulated sugar
4 oz (125 gm) light brown sugar
2 oz (50 gm) golden syrup
1 large egg, lightly beaten
6 oz (175 gm) rolled oats
½ teaspoon vanilla extract
4 oz (125 gm) chopped chocolate (milk, dark or white)
2 - 3 oz (50 - 75 gm) chopped walnuts

Preheat oven to 350F/180C/gas mark 4. Mix together the flour and baking powders. In another bowl cream the butter and sugars for about 1 minute on medium speed. Add the eggs gradually whilst beating and then the vanilla and syrup. Beat on a low speed until well incorporated.

Sift in the flour mixture, still beating on a low speed. Fold in the oatmeal, chocolate and nuts.

Spoon onto baking sheets using 2 teaspoons for small, or 4 teaspoons for giant-sized cookies. Flatten the tops slightly with the spoon. The cookies will spread somewhat so place about 2 to 3 inches apart.

Bake in the centre of the oven for 8 to 12 minutes, depending on the size. The cookies are done when they are golden brown but still soft in the centre.

Cool on a wire rack. The cookies will keep in

 34

an airtight container for 1 week but they are at their most delicious on the day of baking.

Chef's tip:
☆ Pecans, unsalted peanuts or cashews can replace the walnuts.

CHOCOLATE GARNISHES

Working with chocolate requires a little practice but the resulting finishing touches will lend a professional and eye-catching finish to any desserts.

Note: If using couverture, the chocolate will require tempering (see page 4).

GRATED CHOCOLATE

Useful as a very quick garnish, e.g. sprinkling on a plate or decorating a frosted cake.
   Use the coarse-bladed side of a metal grater.

CHOCOLATE CURLS

Use a vegetable peeler to peel off curls from the side of room-temperature chocolate.

CHOCOLATE CARAQUE

Caraque gives a most professional finish to dishes. Piled onto a cake, mounded on a mousse or just 2 or 3 in a contrasting colour to set off a dessert.

 36

Melt a few ounces of chocolate and pour it onto a smooth, clean surface (marble or stainless steel is ideal). Use a palette knife to spread it about ¼ inch (0.6 cm) thick and leave to set completely.

Using a large, sharp straight-bladed knife, hold the blade at a 45 degree angle to the chocolate surface and push gently across the chocolate to form thin scroll-like curls.

Room temperature is ideal for this procedure.

If the chocolate is too cold it will become brittle and break easily. Once made, store carefully as caraque is very delicate.

CHOCOLATE PIPING

Chocolate can be piped directly onto desserts or onto silicone paper to be used as a garnish. You will need greaseproof paper to fashion a piping bag from, and for really professional-looking work, a metal or plastic writing or decorative tip (available in many sizes from cake decorating stores or catering equipment suppliers).

Melt a small amount of chocolate with a few drops of glycerine.

Cut a 4 inch (10 cm) greaseproof paper square and fold it into a cone. Secure it with a piece of sticky-tape. Cut off the tip of the cone and fit the writing tip. Fill the cone two-thirds full and close the back end to fully enclose the filling. If you have no writing tip, fill the cone, and just prior to use snip a tiny hole at the cone's end.

DECORATIVE IDEAS

The simplest method is to pipe geometric patterns onto silicone paper. To ensure that the structure has strength criss-cross the piping to hold it together.

Draw enclosed shapes, e.g., stars or daisies, onto plain paper and overlay it with silicone. Pipe onto the paper following the shape underneath and then fill in the shape with filigree-style squiggles. Leave to set completely.

When ready to use, peel the paper carefully from the designs.

 38

Piping directly onto desserts:

Melted chocolate is fine for piping onto top sur-faces, either as a thin line-writing or drawing or as a line of beading or dots.

Chocolate leaves:

Search out leaves with interesting shapes and textures - holly, rose, mint, etc. Wipe or rinse the leaves and leave to dry before painting the un-derside, quite thickly, with melted chocolate. Once set, carefully peal the leaf away.

Dipping chocolate:

Fruits part-dipped in chocolate make a delicious and attractive garnish, or even a dish by itself - imagine a plate of bitter-chocolate dipped, ripe strawberries and a chilled glass of demi-sec Champagne.

Nuts can be partly or entirely dipped and once cooled, stored in an airtight container for sever-al days.

Dip the fruits, holding the stem - or the nuts, impaled on a sturdy sewing needle - and leave on silicone paper to set.

Chocolate cups:

Paint the inside of paper truffle cases quite thick-ly with melted chocolate. Allow to cool completely and then carefully peel away the paper. Fill the cups with chocolate ganache (see page 42) or a little sweetened whipped cream, topped with a ripe strawberry or a few smaller berries (raspberries, blueberries etc.). A novel idea is to serve the cups with coffee filled with single cream. The entire cup and cream can be stirred into the hot coffee.

CHOCOLATE DACQUOISE

Serves: 4
Preparation time: meringue - 20 minutes, fillings - 15 minutes
Cooking time: meringue - 3 hours
Setting time: ganache - 3 hours
Suitable for dinner party: yes
Suitable for freezing: no
Special equipment: silicone paper, food processor

This is my kind of dessert. Small and light with interesting textures and a bit of decadence. Hazelnut meringue discs are layered with deep, chocolate ganache and airy vanilla whipped cream.

 41

Meringues:
3 large or 4 small egg whites
pinch of cream of tartar
4 oz (125 gm) sugar
2 oz (50 gm) hazelnuts

Ganache:
3 oz (75 gm) dark chocolate, chopped finely
6 oz (175 gm) whipping or double cream
2 tablespoons brandy or rum

Vanilla cream:
8 fl oz (225 ml) whipping cream, chilled
½ teaspoon vanilla extract
2 teaspoons confectioners' sugar

To make the *meringues*. Toast the nuts in a dry sauté pan over a medium heat, shaking often, or in a medium oven until fragrant and golden-brown. Wrap the nuts in a clean tea towel and rub gently to remove the skins. Grind the skinned nuts quite finely.

In a clean bowl beat the whites until frothy, add the cream of tartar and continue beating until soft peaks form. Add half the sugar and beat until stiff peaks form. Add the rest of the sugar and beat on a slow speed until shiny and quite stiff. Fold in the ground nuts.

Either pipe or spoon 12 meringue discs (about 3 inch (7.5 cm) across and ½ inch (1.25 cm) deep) onto silicone paper on baking sheets.

Bake in a preheated 100F/40C/gas mark almost zero oven for 1 hour. Turn off the oven and leave to dry for 2 to 3 hours or overnight until the meringues are crisp and no moisture remains.

Carefully peel away the paper and store the meringues in an airtight container.

For the *ganache*. Scald half of the cream by bringing just to the boil, turning off and remove from the heat immediately. Pour over the chopped chocolate whisking until fully melted and smooth, add the rum or brandy and chill for 2 to 3 hours.

Whip the remaining cream until soft peaks form. Beat the chilled chocolate until fluffy. Fold the cream into the chocolate. Store chilled.

To make the *vanilla cream*. Whip all the ingredients until soft peaks form. Store chilled.

43

To serve:

☆ Place a ½ teaspoon of the cream in the centre of 4 plates - as an anchor - and set a meringue on each blob. Spread the meringue with ganache approximately two-thirds of an inch (1.75 cm) thick and top with another meringue. Mound a tablespoon or so of vanilla cream onto the second meringue and top with a third meringue disc.

Dust the top and the rim of the plate with cocoa powder or decorate with a few caraques or curls (see page 36).

Chef's tips:

☆ The meringues can be made several days in advance and stored in an airtight container. If you prefer plain meringues the nuts can be omitted.

☆ The ganache can be made up to 3 days before and store covered in the fridge. Remove from refrigerator 1 hour before assembly.

☆ Fresh berries make a tasty partner to this dessert and can be folded into the cream for the top layer or used to garnish the plate.

44

CHOCOLATE TRUFFLES AND OTHER GOODIES

Makes: lots
Preparation time: 5 - 10 minutes
Cooking time: 5 minutes
Setting time: 3 hours
Assembly time: 30 minutes
Suitable for dinner party: yes
Suitable for freezing: yes
Special equipment: none

As a special gift for a friend or a finale to a special dinner these sweetmeats are easy and fun to make and store well for a week or so in an airtight container. Use your imagination to vary the flavours and additions to the basic recipe.

 45

| 10 oz (275 gm) best quality dark chocolate |
| 2 fl oz (50 ml) double cream |
| 3 egg yolks |
| 3 oz (75 gm) unsalted butter, softened |
| 2 - 3 tablespoons rum, brandy, eau-de-vie or liqueur of choice |
| cocoa powder, toasted coconut, chopped toasted nuts, chocolate vermicelli . . . |

 46

Melt the chocolate in a double boiler.

Heat the cream and yolks in a saucepan over a low heat, stirring constantly, until the mixture thickens slightly. Do not allow to boil. Remove from the heat.

Stir the chocolate into the cream and beat in the butter a little at a time and then the alcohol until fully incorporated. Transfer the mixture to a container and chill covered until firm, about 3 hours.

At this stage the truffle mix can be held in the fridge for 10 days or frozen until required. Defrost overnight in the fridge.

Assembly: Spoon some cocoa powder into a shallow dish. Scoop a teaspoon of truffle mixture and lightly roll into a ball, and then roll in the cocoa powder to coat completely. Continue making truffles using coating mixtures of choice.

The truffles can be stored, chilled, in an airtight container until required.

TOBLERONE MOUSSE
AND FRUIT DIPPERS

Serves: 4
Preparation time: 15 minutes
Assembly time: 10 minutes
Suitable for dinner party: yes
Suitable for freezing: no
Special equipment: none

This mousse is ridiculously easy to make, is full of calories and cholesterol and tastes just marvellous. We make it as a late summer dessert to take advantage of the masses of ripe summer fruits available. We have made the mousse with all three of the Toblerone bars - white, milk and dark - and in our opinion the milk chocolate works best.

 48

7 oz (200 gm) bar Toblerone
8 fl oz (225 ml) double or whipping cream
Fresh, seasonal fruit - berries, bananas, grapes, etc.

Melt the Toblerone bar and allow to cool to tepid but still liquid.

Whip the cream just to the soft peak stage.

Fold in the chocolate. Chill, covered, until needed.

☆ ☆ ☆

 49

To serve:

☆ Prepare fruit. Peel if necessary and cut into bite-sized pieces. Scoop a portion of mousse into a sundae glass and surround with fruit pieces. Serve with a small fork and dip the fruit pieces in the mousse like a fondue.

CHOCOLATE DELICE

Serves: 10
Preparation time: base - 15 minutes, topping - 15 minutes
Cooking time: 10 minutes
Setting time: 2 hours
Suitable for dinner party: yes
Suitable for freezing: yes
Special equipment: 9 or 10 inch (22.5 or 25 cm) springform cake tin, silicone paper

A chewy, fudgy base and an airy, creamy topping. Simple and quick to make and a delicious dessert or treat with coffee. It also freezes beautifully.

 51

Chocolate fudge base:
2 oz (50 gm) butter
2 oz (50 gm) brown sugar
1½ oz (40 gm) light flour
1½ oz (40 gm) cocoa powder
1 large egg, beaten
1 oz (25 gm) pecans or walnuts, chopped
½ teaspoon vanilla extract
Delice topping:
11 oz (300 gm) dark chocolate, chopped
½ leaf gelatin
16 fl oz (450 ml) whipping cream

To make the *fudge base* preheat the oven to 350F / 180C / gas mark 4. Cut silicone paper to fit the springform pan.

Melt the butter in a saucepan. Remove from the heat and immediately add sugar and cocoa powder and mix thoroughly. Let cool slightly before beating in the egg. Stir in the sifted flour, nuts and vanilla and spread the mixture in the pan and bake for 8 to 10 minutes until just firm.

Allow to cool in the pan.

For the *topping,* soak the gelatin leaf in a little cold water for 5 minutes.

Melt the chocolate and beat in the softened gelatin leaf until fully dissolved. Whip the cream until stiff peaks just form. Be careful not to over-whip.

Fold the cream thoroughly into the cooled chocolate then spread the mixture over the base in the pan. Smooth the top and freeze the des-

52

sert for 2 hours to set or up to a week until required. (If fully frozen, defrost in refrigerator for 4 hours or more.)

To serve:
☆ Run a knife around the inside of the pan before releasing the springform. Garnish the delice by pressing shaved chocolate onto the sides and perhaps piping a design on the top (see page 36).

Chef's tip:
☆ For a special dinner party presentation you could make individual Chocolate Delice Tart-

 53

lets. Cut silicone paper to fit the bottom of ramekins or flat-topped dariole moulds. Fill the
moulds almost to the top with the chocolate
mixture and top with fudge base circles cut to
fit. Wrap and freeze until a few hours before
serving. Defrost in the fridge and run a thin,
flexible bladed knife around the inside of the
mould to release the mini-Delice.

Place the dessert in the centre of a plate and
garnish with caraque or curls and fresh or
puréed fruit.

APRICOT AND CHOCOLATE BRIOCHE

Serves: 6
Preparation time: 25 minutes
Cooking time: 25 minutes
Setting time: 15 minutes
Suitable for dinner party: yes
Suitable for freezing: no
Special equipment: baking sheet, 6 soufflé
   dishes or ramekins, whisk, bowl

An interesting twist to a traditional favourite.

 55

6 - 7 oz (175 - 200 gm) brioche, 1 day old	
6 ripe apricots	
2 oz (50 gm) butter, melted	
4 large eggs	
16 fl oz (450 ml) whole milk	
6 oz (175 gm) castor sugar	
1½ teaspoons vanilla	
1 fl oz (25 ml) chocolate or coffee liqueur	
8 oz (225 gm) chocolate, finely chopped	
Topping:	
2 teaspoons granulated sugar	
1 teaspoon cinnamon	

Preheat oven to 325F/160C/gas mark 3. Cut the brioche into ¾ inch (1.75 cm) cubes. Blanch, peel, and pit the apricots and cut into cubes of one-

third of an inch (0.85 cm).

Butter 6 small soufflé dishes or ramekins.

Toss the brioche with the melted butter in a bowl. Spread the cubes in a single layer on a baking sheet and toast in the oven until a light, golden colour.

In a large bowl whisk together the eggs, milk, sugar, vanilla and liqueur for 2 minutes. Stir in the brioche, apricot and chocolate. Divide between the ramekins.

Combine the granulated sugar and cinnamon and sprinkle it over the ramekins.

Bake for 20 to 25 minutes until puffed and barely set.

The puddings should stand for 10 minutes before serving.

To serve:
☆ Serve in the ramekins and garnish with a little sweetened whipped cream.

Chef's tips:
☆ This can also be made as one large pudding. Use a 7 - 9 inch (17.5 - 22.5 cm) straight-sided dish and adjust baking time as necessary (slightly longer for a deeper pudding).
☆ Brioche gives the puddings a luxurious, light, but rich texture. However, unsliced white bread works equally well. Use day-old bread rather than fresh.
☆ Peaches or nectarines also work well in this recipe.

GEOFF'S CHOCOLATE CHEESECAKE

Serves: 12
Preparation time: 15 minutes
Cooking time: 40 - 45 minutes
Setting time: 1 hour
Suitable for dinner party: yes
Suitable for freezing: no
Special equipment: 10 inch (25 cm) springform pan, food processor, silicone paper

This is a drop-dead, easy, perfect-every-time, sumptuous dessert that Geoff has been making for many years. During the winter it is a feature dessert at the restaurant and Geoff amazes staff and customers by dreaming up a new cheese-cake each day. Use your imagination and adapt this basic recipe to suit your taste with the addi-tion of ground or toasted nuts, fruit purée, chocolate flakes or chips, caramel, 2 chocolates swirled, fudge, the list is endless . . .

Cookie crumb base:
5 oz (150 gm) digestive biscuits
1 tablespoon sugar
1½ oz (40 gm) butter, melted
Cheesecake filling:
8 oz (225 gm) chocolate, chopped
2 lb 4 oz (1 kg) full fat cream cheese
4 whole eggs
0 - 2 oz sugar*

To make the *base,* preheat the oven to 350F/180C/gas mark 4. Cut silicone paper to fit the springform pan.

Break the biscuits into the food processor and process on a slow speed to crumbs with the sugar and then place the crumbs in a bowl.

Melt the butter and mix into the crumbs. Press the mixture into the base of the springform pan and bake in a 350F/180C/gas mark 4 oven for about 10 minutes to set the crust.

For the *filling* melt the chocolate and allow to cool somewhat. Clean the food processor.

Mix the cream cheese and eggs in the food processor until smooth. Add the chocolate (and sugar if necessary) with the motor running, and continue processing until fully incorporated.

Pour the mixture onto the base and bake for 45 to 50 minutes. (The cake should be set around the edges but not in the centre.) Turn off the oven and leave the cake in the oven for 15 minutes more then remove from the oven and leave to cool completely. The cake will continue to set as it cools.

 59

To serve:
☆ Run a thin-bladed knife around the inside of the pan before removing the springform sides. Serve with fresh berries and a little crème fraîche or whipped cream.

Chef's tips:
☆ *adjust the sugar quantity according to the

sweetness of the chocolate used. White chocolate may be sweet enough without additional
sugar.

☆ This cake will keep for a week, covered and
refrigerated.

 61

OLD-STYLE CHOCOLATE FUDGE SAUCE

Makes: about 12 fl oz (350 ml)
Preparation time: 5 minutes
Cooking time: 10 minutes
Suitable for freezing: yes
Special equipment: heavy-based saucepan

Great for drizzling over ice cream or just about any dessert I can think of.

 62

4 oz (125 gm) butter	
8 oz (225 gm) dark chocolate, chopped	
4 oz (125 gm) soft brown sugar	
2 teaspoons instant coffee	
4 fl oz (125 ml) whipping cream	
5 fl oz (150 ml) evaporated milk	
1½ teaspoons vanilla extract	

Melt the butter and the chocolate, slowly, in a saucepan.

Add the sugar, coffee, cream and milk and bring to a boil, stirring constantly. Turn down the heat and simmer, still stirring, for 5 minutes.

Remove from the heat and add vanilla.

Chef's tip:
☆ The sauce will keep well in the fridge, covered, for up to 10 days. Reheat in a microwave on full power for 20 seconds or in the top of a double boiler.

DARK CHOCOLATE PÂTÉ STUDDED WITH WHITE CHOCOLATE CHIPS

Serves: 12
Preparation time: 45 minutes - 1 hour
Setting time: several hours
Suitable for dinner party: yes
Suitable for freezing: yes
Special equipment: terrine dish 10 x 4 x 3 inches (25 x 10 x 7.5 cm), plastic wrap or silicone paper

This is a sinful and decadent dessert for real chocoholics only. It has a rich, silk-like texture with crunchy, melt-in-the-mouth white chocolate throughout.

We use Valrhona chocolate (70%) for the ultimate chocolate high, but you will achieve excellent results with any high quality chocolate with over 50% cocoa solids.

 65

1 lb (450 gm) very best quality dark chocolate, chopped
5 oz (150 gm) castor sugar
3 large egg whites
8 large egg yolks
6 oz (175 gm) butter
4 oz (125 gm) white chocolate, chopped into small pieces
Chocolate coating:
6 oz (175 gm) dark chocolate, chopped
1½ oz (40 gm) butter
1 tablespoon glucose syrup
4 fl oz (125 ml) whipping cream

Cream the yolks and 4 oz (125 gm) of the sugar until doubled in volume, for about 5 minutes. Melt the dark chocolate and the butter in a largish bowl over a pan of barely-simmering water. As soon as the mixture becomes liquid, add the beaten egg mix to the melted chocolate and stir over the heat, until the mixture becomes shiny and somewhat thicker - about 5 minutes.

Remove the bowl from the heat and leave to cool.

Meanwhile in a clean bowl, beat the egg whites until soft peaks form, add the remaining 1 oz (25 gm) of sugar and continue beating until shiny and stiff.

Whisk a quarter of the egg white into the cooled chocolate mixture then carefully fold the remaining whites into the chocolate using a metal spoon.

Line the terrine dish with plastic wrap or sil-

 66

icone paper, leaving a generous overhang to fold over the top.

Using a large ladle, spoon a half to two-thirds of an inch (1.25 to 1.85 cm) layer of the pâté mixture into the terrine dish.

Sprinkle a quarter of the chopped white chocolate evenly over the dark chocolate.

Repeat the layers of chocolate pâté and chopped white chocolate and finish with a layer of dark chocolate.

 67

Carefully fold the plastic wrap or silicone paper over the top of the terrine dish and freeze the terrine for 4 hours or until needed.

To glaze the pâté: Defrost at room temperature for approximately 1 hour before easing the wrapped pâté from the terrine dish. Turn upside down onto a wire rack. Stand the rack over a baking sheet or tray. Carefully peel off the wrapping.

Melt all the chocolate coating ingredients in a metal bowl over barely-simmering water or the top of a double boiler, stir until smooth, remove from heat and allow to cool almost to room temperature.

Ladle the chocolate glaze slowly over the pâté, working from one end to the other and allowing the glaze to coat the sides.

Leave in a cool area to set then carefully lift the pâté onto a serving plate or tray. Refrigerate until needed.

To serve:
☆ Using a large knife with a thin blade, cut a portion-sized slice and place in the centre of the plate. Garnish with fresh raspberries or strawberries and a little crème fraîche.

Chef's tips:
☆ Once the glaze has set, cover tightly with plastic wrap and this dessert will keep well for over a week in the fridge.
☆ As it is the main ingredient, the quality of chocolate used for the pâté is extremely important. Use the very best available.

 68

☆ Instead of white chocolate you could use finely chopped pistachio nuts or, alternatively, raisins, chopped coarsely and soaked in dark rum for several hours.

DARK CHOCOLATE & ORANGE SORBET

Serves: 4
Preparation time: 25 minutes
Cooking time: 5 minutes
Waiting/freezing time: 3 hours
Suitable for dinner party: yes
Special equipment: sorbet/ice cream machine*

A chocolate dessert without guilt! All the flavour and minimal calories. Use the very best
quality chocolate available.

 70

1 lb (450 gm) dark chocolate, very finely chopped
6 oz (175 gm) sugar
14 fl oz (400 ml) water
grated zest (peel) of 1 orange
1 teaspoon sugar

Bring the water and sugar to a boil and simmer, stirring until the sugar is completely melted.

Remove from the heat and immediately add the chocolate, whisking until it is fully incorporated.

Set aside to cool, then refrigerate, covered, for at least 1 hour.

Using a pestle and mortar or the back of a spoon, grind together the orange peel and the teaspoon of sugar and add it to the cooled chocolate mixture.

Process in an ice cream maker according to the manufacturer's instructions.

To serve:
☆ Serve on a puddle of puréed berries (strained), with a few fresh berries, with the Orange Sauce (page 23) or, for real chocoholics - on a pool of Chocolate Fudge Sauce (see page 62)

Chef's tip:
☆ Water is an important ingredient in this recipe. If your tap water is less than pure and

 71

sweet-tasting, invest in a bottle of still mineral water to ensure the best results.

☆ The orange zest is optional but we like the way it lifts the chocolate flavours.

☆ *If you do not own a 'sorbet maker' this can still be made quite successfully by freezing the mixture in a shallow plastic or stainless steel container and by beating the mixture with a hand whisk once it has begun to freeze. Continue to beat each half hour until the sorbet is quite firm.

CHOCOLATE ICE CREAM

Serves: 6
Preparation time: 20 minutes
Cooling & freezing time: 2 to 3 hours
Suitable for dinner party: yes
Special equipment: heavy-bottomed saucepan, ice cream/sorbet maker, double boiler

 73

7 oz (200 gm) chocolate, chopped
6 oz (175 gm) sugar
7 egg yolks
7 fl oz (200 ml) cream, whipping or double
1 pint (550 ml) milk
½ teaspoon vanilla extract
2 - 3 tablespoons rum, brandy or coffee liqueur, optional

Melt the chocolate in the top of a double boiler.

Scald the milk and cream in a saucepan. Meanwhile whisk together the yolks and sugar in a bowl. Pour a little of the hot milk and cream mixture over the eggs whilst beating to incorporate, and then pour the tempered egg mixture

back into the saucepan. Return to a moderate heat, stirring constantly until the mixture thickens slightly (175F/80C on a sugar thermometer) and coats the spoon. Do not allow to boil. Remove immediately from the heat and continue stirring until it has cooled slightly.

Whisk about a cupful into the melted chocolate then stir in the vanilla, alcohol (if using) and the remaining custard.

Allow to cool thoroughly before freezing in an ice cream maker following the manufacturer's instructions.

 75

CHOCOLATE SOUFFLÉS

Serves: 4
Preparation time: 15 minutes
Cooking time: 20 minutes
Suitable for dinner party: yes
Suitable for freezing: no
Special equipment: soufflé dishes or large rame-
  kins

People with little cooking experience are totally intimidated by soufflés, yet they are actually a breeze to make - inexpensive, light, delicious and terribly impressive as a dinner party finale.

 76

7 oz (200 gm) chocolate, melted	
8 oz (225 ml) full fat milk	
1 oz (25 gm) self-raising flour, sifted	
3 large eggs, separated	
1 oz (25 gm) butter	
melted butter and sugar to coat dishes	

Pouring sauce (optional):

4 fl oz (125 ml) whipping cream	
1 fl oz (25 ml) orange-based liqueur (Grand Marnier, Cointreau, Triple Sec etc.)	
grated zest (peel) of 1 well-scrubbed orange	

Prepare the *sauce* by lightly whipping the cream and stirring in the liqueur and grated peel (it should be thickened but still pourable). Reserve, chilled.

For the *soufflés*. Preheat oven to 350F / 180C / gas mark 4. Brush the insides of the soufflé dishes with melted butter and coat with castor sugar.

Melt the butter and mix in the flour, beating well until incorporated.

In another saucepan scald the milk, pour it into the first pan and beat the mixture over medium heat for about 2 minutes. The mixture will thicken somewhat.

Transfer to a bowl and beat in the melted chocolate and egg yolks.

In the other bowl beat the egg whites until stiff peaks form. Carefully fold into the chocolate mixture.

Divide into the prepared soufflé dishes and bake 20 minutes or until well risen.

To serve:
☆ Remove to serving plates, sprinkle with confectioners' sugar and serve immediately with a jug of sauce on the table for all to share.

Sources of high-quality chocolate:

The Chocolate Society
Norwood Bottom Farm
Norwood Bottom
Otley
West Yorkshire LS21 2RA
01943-851101
Operates mail order.

Vin Sullivan Foods
Triley Mill
Abergavenny
Gwent NP7 8DE
01873 852331
Mail order: 1 kilo/2.2lb minimum order
plus postage and packing.

In the same series:

Others in preparation!